The READY RESOURCE *for* RELIEF SOCIETY

The READY RESOURCE for RELIEF SOCIETY

Volume One

TEACHINGS OF PRESIDENTS OF THE CHURCH:
WILFORD WOODRUFF

compiled by
KIMBERLY S. SHAFFER

CFI
Springville, Utah

© 2005 Kimberly S. Shaffer

All rights reserved.

No part of this book may be reproduced in any form whatsoever, whether by graphic, visual, electronic, film, microfilm, tape recording, or any other means, without prior written permission of the author, except in the case of brief passages embodied in critical reviews and articles.

ISBN: 1-55517-921-5
v.1

Published by CFI,
an imprint of Cedar Fort, Inc.
925 N. Main, Springville, Utah, 84663
www.cedarfort.com

Distributed by:

Cover and book design by Nicole Williams
Cover design © 2005 by Lyle Mortimer

Printed in the United States of America
10 9 8 7 6 5 4 3 2 1

Printed on acid-free paper.

DEDICATION

To Momert, who always took me to church.

CONTENTS

Acknowledgments ix
Lesson One 1
Lesson Two 7
Lesson Three 13
Lesson Four 19
Lesson Five 25
Lesson Six 31
Lesson Seven 37
Lesson Eight 43
Lesson Nine 49
Lesson Ten 55
Lesson Eleven 61
Lessson Twelve 67
Lesson Thirteen 73
Lesson Fourteen 79
Lesson Fifteen 85
Lesson Sixteen 91
Lesson Seventeen 97
Lesson Eighteen 103
Lesson Nineteen 109
Lesson Twenty 115
Lesson Twenty-One 121
Lesson Twenty-Two 127
Lesson Twenty-Three 133
Lesson Twenty-Four 139
About the Author 144

ACKNOWLEDGMENTS

Thanks to Michael Morris and Mindy Higginson for their editing, Nikki Williams for the cover, the staff at Cedar Fort for publishing this book, and, most important, my family.

LESSON ONE

THE RESTORATION OF THE GOSPEL

Hymns

No. 34, "Teach Me to Walk in the Light"
No. 283, "The Glorious Gospel Light Has Shone"
No. 2, "The Spirit of God"

SUMMARY:

1. The gospel of Jesus Christ is everlasting and unchanging. In many different dispensations, the Lord has established His kingdom on the earth. Each prophet taught and teaches the same principles of the gospel. There is only one gospel, and there will always only be one gospel.

2. The church that Jesus Christ established during His mortal ministry is the same that was restored through the Prophet Joseph Smith. Christ brought the gospel to the Jews and established His kingdom during His earthy ministry. Over time, the kingdom of God was taken from the earth, and nearly all the men who officiated in the Church were put to death. The same organization and gospel that Christ established was restored through Joseph Smith.

3. We now have the privilege of walking in the light of the restored gospel. We as Latter-day Saints are blessed to have the knowledge

of the restored gospel. We have the restored truth to guide and direct our lives. With the light of the gospel, we can begin to understand the mercy and love of our Savior and our Father in Heaven.

QUOTES:

"The Church of Jesus Christ of Latter-day Saints is also in the unique position of knowing that there were different gospel dispensations. These dispensations began with Adam. One scripture says, 'And thus the Gospel began to be preached, from the beginning, being declared by holy angels sent forth from the presence of God, and by his own voice, and by the gift of the Holy Ghost' (Moses 5:58)" (Neal A. Maxwell, "The Wondrous Restoration," *Ensign*, April 2003, 35).

"Yes, the Restoration has brought to earth again the true doctrines and ordinances of the gospel of Jesus Christ. The Restoration affects every fiber of our being. It consumes every part of our mortal journey. It keeps us focused on which path we should walk upon in our daily search for meaning to life. There truly is a strait and narrow path that leads to eternal life by following the Savior and the living prophets. *We must accept them as the inspired trainers for our race of life*" (Gary J. Coleman, "Jesus Christ Is at the Center of the Restoration of the Gospel," *Ensign*, November 1992, 44).

"I pray that we each will see how great the importance is to gain an understanding, through diligent and prayerful study, of the divine Sonship of Jesus Christ—the Savior of the world; that Joseph Smith's divine mission was to bring about the restoration of the principles and ordinances of the gospel of Jesus Christ, and also the Book of Mormon, which is indeed another witness that Jesus Christ is the Son of the living God; and that this church—The Church of Jesus Christ of Latter-day Saints—is 'the Lord's kingdom once again established on the earth, preparatory to the second coming of the Messiah' (Introduction, Book of Mormon)" (Robert E. Wells, "Our Message to the World," *Ensign*, November 1995, 66).

NOTES:

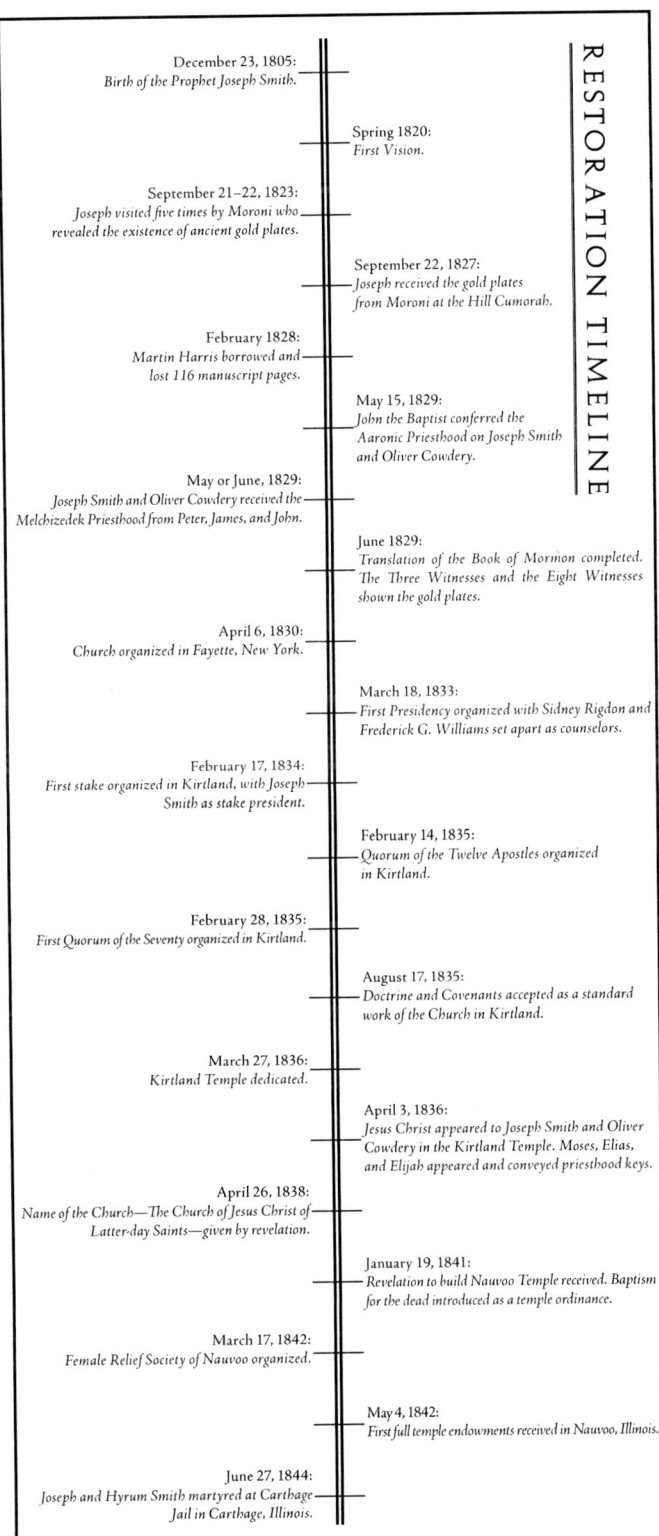

LESSON TWO

JOSEPH SMITH: PROPHET, SEER, AND REVELATOR

No. 27, "Praise to the Man"
No. 21, "Come, Listen to a Prophet's Voice"
No. 19, "We Thank Thee, O God, for a Prophet"

SUMMARY:

1. Joseph Smith was taught by God the Father, Jesus Christ, the Holy Ghost, and angels from heaven. The Prophet was a farmer's son with little to no education. He brought about the restoration of the gospel and the priesthood, as well as the translation of the Book of Mormon, through inspiration and guidance from Heavenly Father and Jesus Christ. The power of revelation and inspiration was with him each day as he led and guided the newly formed Church.

2. With a vision of the Church's destiny, Joseph Smith prepared the apostles to carry on the work of the Church. Joseph spent months and months teaching the apostles. Inspired of the Lord, the Prophet bestowed the keys and the authority of the priesthood upon the apostles.

3. Joseph Smith remained true to his testimony despite trials and persecutions, and he sealed his testimony with his blood. The Prophet met persecution and opposition from the world every day;

it would have been easy for many to give up and to renounce the truth. Joseph Smith stayed firm and true to the gospel, not once denying its truth. The shedding of his blood was the last testimony he gave to this dispensation.

QUOTES:

"I look with wonder at the life of Joseph Smith, a farm boy of Palmyra, New York. He had very little schoolbook education. He knew little of the classroom. His opportunity for reading was severely restricted. But as an instrument in the hands of the Almighty, he spoke words that have become the law and the testimony of this great, vital work. The Doctrine and Covenants is a conduit for the expressions of the Lord to his people" (Gordon B. Hinckley, "The Order and Will of God," *Ensign*, January 1989, 4).

"Joseph Smith placed commitment ahead of life itself. From the time of his first vision until his martyrdom, he was a victim of bitter persecution, reviling, and ridicule, but never did he falter in spite of extreme adversity. As he recorded his story, he wrote:

'However, it was nevertheless a fact that I had beheld a vision. I have thought since, that I felt much like Paul, when he made his defense before King Agrippa, and related . . . when he saw a light, and heard a voice; but still there were but few who believed him; some said he was dishonest, others said he was mad; . . . But all this did not destroy the reality of his vision. He had seen a vision, he knew he had. . . .

'So it was with me. I had actually seen a light, and in the midst of that light I saw two Personages, and they did in reality speak to me; and though I was hated and persecuted for saying that I had seen a vision, yet it was true; . . . For I had seen a vision; I knew it, and I knew that God knew it, and I could not deny it, neither dared I do it; at least I knew that by so doing I would offend God, and come under condemnation'

(Joseph Smith–History 1:24–25)" (Marvin J. Ashton, "The Word Is Commitment," *Ensign*, November 1983, 62).

"Why was Joseph Smith able to do that which was beyond his personal capacity? It was because of his powerful testimony. That led to his obedience, his faith in the Master, and his unwavering determination to do His will. I testify that as your testimony grows in strength, when needed and earned, you can enjoy inspiration to know what to do and when necessary, divine power or capacity to accomplish it. Joseph Smith perfected his ability to follow the guidance of the Lord by practiced personal discipline. He did not let his own desires, convenience, or the persuasions of men interfere with that compliance. Follow his example" (Richard G. Scott, "The Power of a Strong Testimony," *Ensign*, November 2001, 88–89).

NOTES:

I saw two Personages, AND THEY DID IN REALITY SPEAK TO ME; AND THOUGH I WAS HATED AND PERSECUTED FOR SAYING THAT I HAD SEEN A VISION, YET IT WAS TRUE. . . . I KNEW IT, AND I KNEW THAT GOD KNEW IT, AND I COULD NOT DENY IT (JOSEPH SMITH–HISTORY 1:25).

LESSON THREE

THE DISPENSATION OF THE FULNESS OF TIMES

No. 36, "They, the Builders of the Nation"
No. 106, "God Speed the Right"
No. 41, "Let Zion in Her Beauty Rise"

SUMMARY:

1. The Lord has looked to this dispensation from before the creation of the world, and nothing can stop the Church from fulfilling its destiny. This last dispensation and the work of the Church are part of a great plan that was ordained from the beginning. God is the author of this gospel, and He holds its work in His hands. The plans for the Church and the taking of the gospel to the ends of the earth will not be stopped.

2. We were reserved in the spirit world to build the kingdom in the last dispensation. We are waging a great battle with Satan and his hosts. This generation of people is the only one to receive the fulness of the gospel, and it is our responsibility to carry on the work of the kingdom in the last days and to prepare for the coming of the Messiah.

3. As Latter-day Saints, we have a great work to do. Our responsibility and special calling is to build up the kingdom of God, share the

gospel with others, and prepare the earth for the return of Jesus Christ. The Lord will not withdraw His hand until the gospel has been preached to all the earth. We must be instruments in spreading the gospel.

QUOTES:

D&C 65:2

"All the forces of evil combined to fight the work the Lord started through Joseph Smith. Words such as persecution, apostasy, betrayal, treachery, expulsion, condemnation, opposition, extermination, and finally martyrdom fill our early histories. And yet the Prophet Joseph Smith's vision never flagged; he knew the work was God's work, and he knew that God would see it through. 'The Standard of Truth has been erected,' he said; 'no unhallowed hand can stop the work from progressing; persecutions may rage, mobs may combine, armies may assemble, calumny may defame, but the truth of God will go forth boldly, nobly, and independent, till it has penetrated every continent, visited every clime, swept every country, and sounded in every ear, till the purposes of God shall be accomplished, and the Great Jehovah shall say the work is done' (*History of the Church*, 4:540)" (Gerald N. Lund, "A Prophet for the Fulness of Times," *Ensign*, January 1997, 54).

"This is the work of the Lord, and He has given it to us. It is our responsibility, our pleasure, and our privilege to carry this work forward. We should so organize ourselves and the work that it will go forward in leaps and bounds" (Spencer W. Kimball, "The Things of Eternity— Stand We in Jeopardy?" *Ensign*, January 1977, 7).

"Our membership in The Church of Jesus Christ of Latter-day Saints is a precious thing; this is the church and kingdom of God. This is the kingdom of God on this earth. This is His work in which we are engaged and there is no more important work in all the world than this work. It concerns the eternal salvation of the sons and daughters of God, those living, those who have lived upon the earth, and those who will yet live. No people have ever been charged with a greater, more inclusive mandate than we have, you and I. Our work, given to us by the Lord, encompasses all of mankind" (Gordon B. Hinckley, *Stand a Little Taller* [Salt Lake City: Eagle Gate, 2001], 102).

"Make room for the Church in your life. Let your knowledge of its doctrine grow. Let your understanding of its organization increase. Let your love for its eternal truths become ever and ever stronger.

"The Church may call upon you to make sacrifice. It may call upon you to give of the very best that you have to offer. There will be no cost in this, because you will discover that it will become an investment that will pay you dividends for as long as you live. The Church is the great reservoir of eternal truth. Embrace it and hold fast to it" (Gordon B. Hinckley, "Life's Obligations," *Ensign*, February 1999, 4).

NOTES:

 *Unto whom I have committed the keys of my kingdom, and a dispensation of the gospel for the last times; and for the fulness of times, in the which I will gather together in one all things, both with are in heaven, and which are on earth.* —D&C 27:13

LESSON FOUR

THE POWER AND AUTHORITY OF THE HOLY PRIESTHOOD

THE READY RESOURCE FOR RELIEF SOCIETY

No. 319, "Ye Elders of Israel"
No. 19, "We Thank Thee, O God, for a Prophet"
No. 258, "O Thou Rock of Our Salvation"

SUMMARY:

1. The authority and power of God is the priesthood. The priesthood is the way God deals with man on earth. The very organization of the Church is endowed with the priesthood, and no man has authority from God to administer to men the ordinances of the gospel unless he has the power of the priesthood.

2. The priesthood should be used for service and the building of the kingdom. Those men who hold the priesthood will be accountable for that responsibility. If the power of the priesthood is abused, the man abusing that power will be brought under condemnation and left in spiritual darkness.

3. If we remain true to our covenants, we will receive the blessings of the priesthood in this life and throughout eternity. Those who have blessings given to them by the holy priesthood are entitled to all blessings that have been promised and conferred upon them so long as they are true to their covenants.

LESSON FOUR

QUOTES:

D&C 121:37

"The priesthood is here. It has been conferred upon us. We act in that authority. We speak as sons of God in the name of Jesus Christ and as holders of this divinely given endowment. We know, for we have seen, the power of this priesthood. We have seen the sick healed, the lame made to walk, and the coming of light and knowledge and understanding to those who have been in darkness" (Gordon B. Hinckley, "Four Cornerstones of Faith," *Ensign*, February 2004, 6).

"The priesthood is not a passive thing. It is an active power. It is ours to enjoy, to exercise for the blessings of others, to magnify by the manner of our lives, and to advance the cause of the Almighty" (Gordon B. Hinckley, *Stand a Little Taller* [Salt Lake City: Eagle Gate, 2001], 137).

"As worthy members, through priesthood power, make sacred covenants with their Father in Heaven, the plan of salvation is revealed and they are endowed with blessings that extend into the eternities. Couples kneel at the temples' altars and, through the authority restored by Elijah, form new and potentially eternal family units. Through the faithfulness of these couples, the very priesthood that binds them together will assist them as they bring children into the world and rear them in righteousness" (Joy Saunders Lundberg, "The Priesthood: God's Gift of Love," *Ensign*, February 1993, 16).

HANDOUT:

Take a few minutes and have your sisters write down the blessings they have received from the priesthood.

NOTES:

What Blessings Have I Received from the Priesthood?

Aaronic Priesthood

Melchizedek Priesthood

LESSON FIVE

THE HOLY GHOST AND PERSONAL REVELATION

Hymns

No. 143, "Let the Holy Spirit Guide"
No. 137, "Testimony"
No. 302, "I Know My Father Lives"

SUMMARY:

1. The greatest gift anyone can receive in mortality is the gift of the Holy Ghost, which bears witness to the truthfulness of the gospel. The Holy Ghost sustains and comforts us through trials, persecution, and temptation. Those Church members who have been baptized have the right to have the Spirit assist them in their lives as well as strengthen their testimonies of the gospel.

2. We need to learn to listen to the still small voice of the Holy Ghost, which guides our lives and prepares us for eternal life. We need to get acquainted with the way the Spirit speaks to us individually so we may heed the counsel and guidance we receive. The Spirit reveals, day by day, the things we need to know and do to benefit our lives. If we live righteously, we can have this guidance with us always.

3. The constant companionship of the Holy Ghost requires constant effort, faithfulness, and righteous living. The Holy Ghost will

not stay with us if we are unclean. We must forsake our sins and live true to our covenants to have the companionship of the Holy Ghost. When we do this, we will know the paths the Lord would have us take.

QUOTES:

"I believe the Spirit of the Holy Ghost is the greatest guarantor of inward peace in our unstable world. It can be more mind-expanding and can make us have a better sense of well-being than any chemical or other earthly substance. It will calm nerves; it will breathe peace to our souls. This Comforter can be with us as we seek to improve. It can function as a source of revelation to warn us of impending danger and also help keep us from making mistakes. It can enhance our natural senses so that we can see more clearly, hear more keenly, and remember what we should remember. It is a way of maximizing our happiness" (James E. Faust, "The Gift of the Holy Ghost—A Sure Compass," *Ensign*, May 1989, 32–33).

"Following baptism, one is confirmed a member of The Church of Jesus Christ of Latter-day Saints in a brief ordinance, during which there is conferred the gift of the Holy Ghost. Thereafter, all through life, men, women, even little children receive the right to inspired direction to guide them in their lives—personal revelation! The Holy Ghost communicates with the spirit through the mind more than through the physical senses. This guidance comes as thoughts, as feelings, through impressions and promptings" (Boyd K. Packer, "Revelation in a Changing World," *Ensign*, November 1989, 14).

"The Holy Ghost will be our constant companion if we submit ourselves to the will of our Father in Heaven, always remembering Him and keeping His commandments" (L. Tom Perry, "That Spirit Which Leadeth to Do Good," *Ensign*, May 1997, 69).

NOTES:

YOU HAVE THE SPIRIT WHEN:

- *You feel happy and peaceful*
- *You are not easily offended*
- *You are helpful and kind to others*
- *You are optimistic*
- *You willingly serve and attend church*
- *You are in control of your appetites and emotions*
- *You are mindful of the Savior*
- *You desire to pray*
- *You attend the temple often*
- *You feel an eagerness to read the scriptures*
- *You strive to live the commandments*

LESSON SIX

TEACHING AND LEARNING BY THE SPIRIT

Hymns

No. 304, "Teach Me to Walk in the Light"
No. 123, "Oh May My Soul Commune with Thee"
No. 113, "Our Savior's Love"

SUMMARY:

1. The Holy Ghost must be our companion when we teach the gospel. We are not capable of edifying and teaching the doctrines of the Church without inspiration and guidance from Heavenly Father. Without the Spirit, we are unable to enlighten others to know what God would have them learn.

2. The gospel of Jesus Christ teaches plain and simple truths. When we teach the gospel, these truths are the most edifying and enlightening. We need to teach the gospel so that we uplift rather than appear to be intelligent or clever. When we teach, we should not speculate upon things we do not understand or know about; others learn best when we teach the simple truths of the gospel.

3. Those learning about the gospel need the Spirit just as much as those teaching it. We will learn more about the gospel when we allow the Spirit to teach us. We need to prepare our hearts and minds before we receive the counsel of the Lord's servants. When

we do this, those teaching will receive the power of the Lord and the inspiration of the Holy Ghost to teach us the things that we need to learn and practice in our lives.

QUOTES:

"The . . . principle of gospel teaching I wish to stress is the Lord's command, quoted earlier, that gospel teachers should 'teach the principles of my gospel . . . as they shall be directed by the Spirit. . . . And if ye receive not the Spirit ye shall not teach' (D&C 42:12–14). It is a gospel teacher's privilege and duty to seek that level of discipleship where his or her teachings will be directed and endorsed by the Spirit rather than being rigidly selected and prearranged for personal convenience or qualifications" (Dallin H. Oaks, "Gospel Teaching," *Ensign*, November 1999, 80).

"Plainness is best comprehended by the humble, the teachable, the intelligent, the wise, and the obedient. Often plain truths are perverted by the pretentious, the crude, the low, the critical, the contentious, the haughty, and the unrighteous. More so than in any other time in our history, there is urgency in today's society for men and women to step forward and teach the gospel of Jesus Christ in the power of plainness. God delights when His truths are taught clearly and understandably with no conspicuous ornamentation. Plainness in life, word, and conduct are eternal virtues" (Marvin J. Ashton, "The Power of Plainness," *Ensign*, May 1977, 66).

"If we have the Spirit of the Lord to guide us, we can teach any person, no matter how well educated, anyplace in the world. The Lord knows more than any of us, and if we are His servants, acting under His Spirit, He can deliver His message of salvation to each and every soul" (Dallin H. Oaks, "Teaching and Learning by the Spirit," *Ensign*, March 1997, 7).

THE READY RESOURCE FOR RELIEF SOCIETY

HANDOUT:

Make this handout into a magnet that your sisters can keep on their refridgerator.

NOTES:

When you visit your assigned members, you bring with you the light of the gospel, the love and Spirit of the Lord.

—Joseph B. Wirthlin, "Valued Companions," Ensign, November 1997.

When you visit your assigned members, you bring with you the light of the gospel, the love and Spirit of the Lord.

—Joseph B. Wirthlin, "Valued Companions," Ensign, November 1997.

When you visit your assigned members, you bring with you the light of the gospel, the love and Spirit of the Lord.

—Joseph B. Wirthlin, "Valued Companions," Ensign, November 1997.

When you visit your assigned members, you bring with you the light of the gospel, the love and Spirit of the Lord.

—Joseph B. Wirthlin, "Valued Companions," Ensign, November 1997.

LESSON SEVEN

THE ATONEMENT OF JESUS CHRIST

THE READY RESOURCE FOR RELIEF SOCIETY

Hymns

No. 193, "I Stand All Amazed"
No. 258, "O Thou Rock of Our Salvation"
No. 112, "Savior, Redeemer of My Soul"

SUMMARY:

1. Christ came to the earth to redeem us from the effects of the Fall in accordance with the Father's will. Heavenly Father sent Jesus Christ to earth for the salvation of those who believe on His name; this was planned before the world was. Man is governed by a celestial law and therefore requires an infinite celestial sacrifice to atone for his disobedience. Christ, being holy and unspotted from the world, is the only one who can redeem mankind.

2. Exaltation comes only through the gift of the Atonement and our obedience to the laws and ordinances of the gospel. Justice must be satisfied whether or not we partake of the Atonement, which can only be done by abiding by the laws of the gospel. Christ's gift allows us to repent so we can be cleansed through His redeeming blood. Faith in Him and repentance are the first two principles of the gospel.

3. Through the Atonement, we can be perfected; no other way

is available for us to be cleansed of our sins. We can only be perfected in Christ, and we must diligently grow and advance in the knowledge of the gospel so we can be found worthy of the Atonement and receive exaltation.

QUOTES:

"The wondrous gift of the Atonement overcomes physical death unconditionally, and it is infinite because it is for all who have lived or will ever live in mortality. Through the Atonement, we are all redeemed from the Fall of Adam and will be resurrected" (Robert D. Hales, "If Thou Wilt Enter into Life, Keep the Commandments," *Ensign*, May 1996, 36).

"Thus we find that it is not sufficient to believe only, but we must also obey the laws and prove by our works and by keeping the commandments that we are worthy of the saving blessings of the Lord's atonement" (N. Eldon Tanner, "God So Loved the World," *Ensign*, April 1982, 4).

"Jesus Christ is the Son of God, who condescended to come into this world of misery, struggle, and pain to touch men's hearts for good, to teach the way of eternal life, and to give Himself as a sacrifice for the sins of mankind. How different, how empty our lives would be without Him. How infinite is our opportunity for exaltation made possible through His redeeming love" (Gordon B. Hinckley, *Stand a Little Taller* [Salt Lake City: Eagle Gate, 2001], 376).

NOTES:

Whether descriptively designated as Creator, Only Begotten Son, Prince of Peace, Advocate, Mediator, Son of God, Savior, Messiah, Author and Finisher of Salvation, King of Kings—I witness that Jesus Christ is the only name under heaven whereby one can be saved! (See D&C 18:23.)

I testify that He is utterly incomparable in what He *is*, what He *knows*, what He has *accomplished*, and what He has *experienced*. Yet, movingly, He calls us His friends. We can trust, worship, and even adore Him without any reservation! . . .

Indeed, we cannot teach Him anything! But we can listen to Him. We can love Him, we can honor Him, we can worship Him! We can keep His commandments, and we can feast upon His scriptures! Yes, we who are so forgetful and even rebellious are never forgotten by Him! We *are* His "work" and His "glory," and He is *never* distracted!

—*Neal A. Maxwell, "'O, Divine Redeemer,'" Ensign, November 1981.*

LESSON EIGHT

UNDERSTANDING DEATH AND RESURRECTION

No. 200, "Christ the Lord Is Risen Today"
No. 292, "O My Father"
No. 286, "Oh, What Songs of the Heart"

SUMMARY:

1. At death, each person's spirit enters the spirit world to continue in the Lord's work until, through the Atonement of Christ, their spirits are reunited with their bodies. Although the death of loved ones is sorrowful, those who are righteous continue a great and noble work on the other side of the veil. Christ, who died to redeem the world, triumphed over death. Through the Atonement, we too can triumph over death and be reunited with the bodies we occupied in mortality.

2. The gospel provides comfort when loved ones pass away, especially in the case of children who die before the age of accountability. Because children are born innocent and blameless before God, they will inherit celestial glory if they pass away before the age of accountability. This is made possible through the Atonement. If we prove faithful and worthy, our children in these circumstances will be reunited with us in the resurrection.

LESSON EIGHT

3. We need to live our lives so that we are prepared to receive the blessings of God when we die. Our time on this earth is our opportunity to improve and grow in the glory of God. We must not procrastinate righteous living and repentance but instead improve our time, talents, and opportunities every day. We can build the kingdom of God on earth each day and prepare to meet God and Jesus Christ in the next life.

QUOTES:

"If we are aware that the spirit world is a real extension of our mortal existence, we are less likely to set our hearts on the treasures of this world" (Dale C. Mouritsen, "The Spirit World, Our Next Home," *Ensign*, January 1977, 50).

"[President Grant] said that he never attended a funeral of a faithful member of the Church without thanking the Lord 'for the gospel of Jesus Christ, and for the comfort and consolation that it gives to us in the hour of sorrow and death'" (*Teachings of Presidents of the Church: Heber J. Grant* [Salt Lake City: The Church of Jesus Christ of Latter-day Saints, 2002], 5).

"Now is the time to prepare. Then, when death comes, we can move toward the celestial glory that Heavenly Father has prepared for His faithful children. Meanwhile, for sorrowing loved ones left behind—such as our family and me—the sting of death is soothed by a steadfast faith in Christ, a perfect brightness of hope, a love of God and of all men, and a deep desire to serve them" (Russell M. Nelson, "Now Is the Time to Prepare," *Ensign*, May 2005, 18).

NOTES:

I remember vividly an experience I had as a passenger in a small two-propeller airplane. One of its engines suddenly burst open and caught on fire. The propeller of the flaming engine was starkly stilled. As we plummeted in a steep spiral dive toward the earth, I expected to die. Some of the passengers screamed in hysterical panic. Miraculously, the precipitous dive extinguished the flames. Then, by starting up the other engine, the pilot was able to stabilize the plane and bring us down safely.

Throughout that ordeal, though I "knew" death was coming, my paramount feeling was that I was not afraid to die. I remember a sense of returning home to meet ancestors for whom I had done temple work. I remember my deep sense of gratitude that my sweetheart and I had been sealed eternally to each other and to our children, born and reared in the covenant. I realized that our marriage in the temple was my most important accomplishment. Honors bestowed upon me by men could not approach the inner peace provided by sealings performed in the house of the Lord.

—Russell M. Nelson, "Doors of Death," *Ensign*, May 1992.

LESSON NINE

PROCLAIMING
THE GOSPEL

THE READY RESOURCE FOR RELIEF SOCIETY

No. 249, "Called to Serve"
No. 41, "Let Zion in Her Beauty Rise"
No. 219, "Because I Have Been Given Much"

SUMMARY:

1. We are responsible for sharing the gospel. As those who have the truth of the gospel, we will be held responsible for what we do with that knowledge. It is our calling and duty from God to declare the words of God to His children. Not only are we responsible to teach the gospel to others, but we are also responsible to teach it in our homes.

2. Great joy comes from helping others come unto Christ and receive the good news of the gospel. We need to become instruments in the Lord's hands. There is no greater calling or privilege than to teach the gospel and save the souls of men. When we teach the gospel, we need to remember that we must not waste our time in tearing down the religion of others. We will be able to better convince and convert by our example.

3. The Lord provides guidance to those who listen to and teach the gospel through the Holy Ghost. The truths of the gospel are

simple and true. When we teach with the Spirit, the Spirit testifies of the truthfulness of those principles. The Lord will go before us and, through the Holy Ghost, prepare the hearts of those who will receive the message of the gospel.

QUOTES:

"Our work is to preach the gospel to the world. It is not self-imposed. We are under divine commandment. The Prophet Joseph Smith said: "After all has been said, the greatest and most important duty is to preach the gospel." All the other programs are extremely important but, of course, we cannot influence people until we get them in the Church" (Spencer W. Kimball, "President Kimball Speaks Out on Being a Missionary," *New Era*, May 1981, 49).

"In no part of the work of God here upon the earth at the present time is there such a band of happy, contented, peaceful people as those who are engaged in missionary service. Service is the real key to joy. When one is giving service for the advancement of humanity, when one is working without money and without price, with no hope of earthly reward, there comes a real, genuine joy into the human heart" (*Teachings of Presidents of the Church: Heber J. Grant* [Salt Lake City: The Church of Jesus Christ of Latter-day Saints, 2002], 9).

"The great need today in missionary work is to have all the members, every member—those who bear His name, those who have had a witness—pull aside the curtains of fear and reach out in love to our friends and relatives and neighbors and let them know that we really care about them and warm them with our love, that they may know that we really do care for them as our brothers and sisters, that they too might enjoy these great blessings" (Rex C. Reeve Sr., "Feed My Sheep," *Ensign*, November 1980, 28).

HANDOUT:

Take a few minutes with your sisters to make a list of how they might teach the gospel everyday.

NOTES:

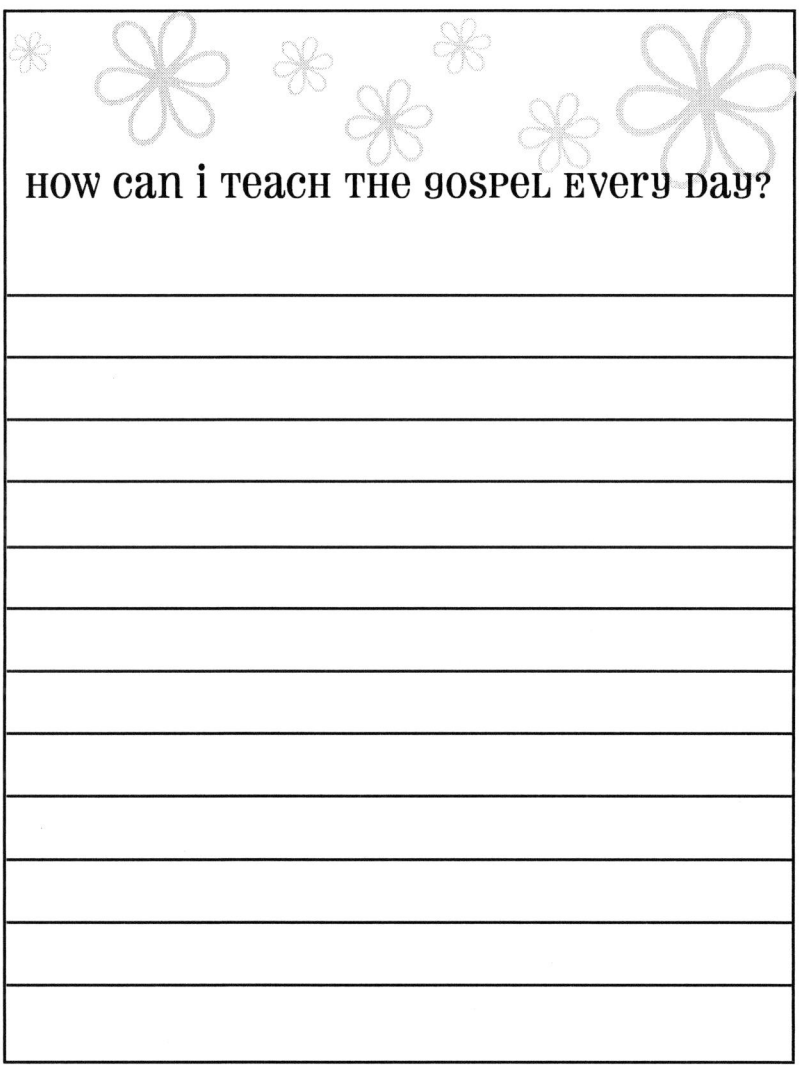

LESSON TEN

HUMBLE RELIANCE ON GOD

Hymns

No. 130, "Be Thou Humble"
No. 98, "I Need Thee Every Hour"
No. 131, "More Holiness Give Me"

SUMMARY:

1. We depend upon God for all spiritual and temporal blessings. We must understand that the Lord's ways are greater than our own. His guidance and counsel may seem to call for too great a sacrifice, but they are always the best and safest course for us to follow. We are entirely dependent upon God for our support, and our blessings are in His hands. When He calls on us to do work and follow His guidance, we must trust Him.

2. The Lord chooses humble and meek servants to do His work; those who become prideful will fall. For example, God chose Moses, who was slow of speech, and Joseph Smith, who was uneducated, to lead His people. God chooses the meek because they are humble and He can make something out of them. We will never see a day on earth or in the world to come when we will not need the protection, care, and support of God. We must be humble, watchful, and prayerful so we can receive these blessings.

LESSON TEN

Pride is something we need to be aware of so we do not fall.

3. When we humbly serve and rely on the Lord, He protects and strengthens us. We all have weaknesses that God has given us so we might be taught to be humble. Those who are humble and rely on God never falter in the fight for righteousness. If we are humble, keep the commandments faithfully, and pray to our Heavenly Father, He will bless and strengthen us.

QUOTES:

"The Lord has given you this glorious Church, His Church, to guide you and direct you, to give you opportunity for growth and experience, to teach you and lead you and encourage you, to make of you His chosen daughter or son, one upon whom He may look with love and with a desire to help. Of course there will be some problems along the way. There will be difficulties to overcome. But they will not last forever. He will not forsake you" (Gordon B. Hinckley, *Stand a Little Taller* [Salt Lake City: Eagle Gate, 2001], 48).

"It has been said that this church does not necessarily attract great people but more often makes ordinary people great. Many nameless people with gifts equal only to five loaves and two small fishes magnify their callings and serve without attention or recognition, feeding literally thousands. In large measure, they make possible the fulfillment of Nebuchadnezzar's dream that the latter-day gospel of Christ would be like a stone cut out of the mountains without hands, rolling forth until it fills the whole earth (see Dan. 2:34–35; D&C 65:2). These are the hundreds of thousands of leaders and teachers in all of the auxiliaries and priesthood quorums, the home teachers, the Relief Society visiting teachers. These are the many humble bishops in the Church, some without formal training but greatly magnified, always learning, with a humble desire to serve the Lord and the people of their wards" (James E.

Faust, "Five Loaves and Two Fishes," *Ensign*, May 1994, 5).

"Humility does not mean weakness. It does not mean timidity; it does not mean fear. A man can be humble and fearless" (Ezra Taft Benson, "Keys to Successful Member-Missionary Work," *Ensign*, September 1990, 5).

NOTES:

Yet as we learn about the workings of God, the power of a humble and submissive spirit becomes apparent. In the kingdom of God, greatness begins with humility and submissiveness. These companion virtues are the first critical steps to opening the doors to the blessings of God and the power of the priesthood.

—*Richard C. Edgley, "Empowerment of Humility," Ensign, November 2003.*

LESSON ELEVEN

PRAYING TO RECEIVE THE BLESSINGS OF HEAVEN

Hymns

No. 140, "Did You Think to Pray"
No. 298, "Home Can Be a Heaven on Earth"
No. 144, "Secret Prayer"

SUMMARY:

1. It is our duty to pray with faith for help, guidance, and understanding of the Lord's will. We do not fully realize the benefits of prayer. God hears and answers the prayers of all people, and the power of prayer can bring the blessings of God almost more than any other thing. If we pray in faith, He will answer our prayers with His counsel and guidance.

2. Parents have the responsibility to teach their children to pray and to hold family prayer. The Lord wants us to teach children who are old enough to pray. We need to teach them to understand the benefits of prayer so they can pray for those things that are necessary.

3. When we are true to our covenants and righteously live the gospel, our prayers will be answered and we will be blessed. We should be humble and submissive when we pray so we may receive the blessings of our Heavenly Father. In addition, we should live our

lives so that we are worthy of those blessings. Only those who pray in faith and follow the will of the Lord will receive His blessings.

QUOTES:

"While the blessings we ask for and receive through prayer are undeniably magnificent, the greatest blessing and benefit is not in the physical blessings that may come as answers to our prayers but in the changes to our souls that come as we learn to be dependent on Heavenly Father for strength" (David E. Sorensen, "Prayer," *Ensign*, May 1993, 31).

"The most important way to teach children to pray is through example. As they hear us pray, so they will learn to pray. Besides family prayer, we can pray with each child alone at various times" ("Teaching Children about Prayer," *Ensign*, January 1989, 60).

"Your prayer can take many forms. It can be sung in a hymn, or whispered, or even thought. It can be as short as one word—'help!'—or it could be as long as Enos's prayer that lasted all night and all day. The important thing to remember is to pray often, talk to Heavenly Father, seek his counsel so that he can guide you. When you draw near to Heavenly Father in prayer, he will draw near to you. You need never feel alone again" (Dwan J. Young, "Draw Near to Him in Prayer," *Ensign*, November 1985, 92).

NOTES:

WAYS TO IMPROVE YOUR PRAYERS

- GET ON YOUR KNEES
- PRAY FOR THE SPIRIT
- PREPARE YOUR HEART, AND PONDER IN ADVANCE
- BE GRATEFUL—START WITH THANK-YOUS
- LISTEN FOR ANSWERS
- PRAY UNTIL YOU HAVE THE DESIRE TO PRAY
- PRAY UNTIL YOU FEEL THE COMPANIONSHIP OF YOUR SAVIOR

LESSON TWELVE

RICH TREASURES
IN THE SCRIPTURES

No. 277, "As I Search the Holy Scriptures"
No. 274, "The Iron Rod"
No. 279, "Thy Holy Word"

SUMMARY:

1. We must study the scriptures and practice the truths we learn from them. It is our duty to contemplate and ponder the truths taught in the scriptures. We can draw closer to the Lord and obtain the Holy Spirit by following His counsel. This will help us to study the scriptures with that same Spirit by which they were written and translated. We must study them in our hearts and practice them in our lives.

2. The Book of Mormon and the Bible join to proclaim the fulness of the gospel, while the Doctrine and Covenants proclaims truths revealed in our day. The Bible contains the law of God through Moses and the ancient prophets. The Book of Mormon was written by apostles and prophets living on the American continent and contains the teachings of Christ when He appeared there. The Doctrine and Covenants shows us what lies before this earth and what awaits this nation and people.

LESSON TWELVE

3. Prophecies in the scriptures can lead and guide us as well as help us prepare for the Second Coming. We need to study the scriptures so we can be prepared for what the Lord has in store for us. Studying the scriptures takes faithfulness and earnest prayer. We need to pray that we will have a correct understanding of what we study.

QUOTES:

"We should make daily study of the scriptures a lifetime pursuit.... One of the most important things you can do ... is to immerse yourselves in the scriptures. Search them diligently.... Learn the doctrine. Master the principles.... You must ... see that studying and searching the scriptures is not a burden laid upon [us] by the Lord, but a marvelous blessing and opportunity" (Ezra Taft Benson, "Godly Characteristics of the Master," *Ensign*, November 1986, 47).

"The Book of Mormon is also the keystone of the doctrine of the resurrection. As mentioned before, the Lord Himself has stated that the Book of Mormon contains the 'fulness of the gospel of Jesus Christ.' (D&C 20:9.) That does not mean it contains every teaching, every doctrine ever revealed. Rather, it means that in the Book of Mormon we will find the fulness of those doctrines required for our salvation. And they are taught plainly and simply so that even children can learn the ways of salvation and exaltation. The Book of Mormon offers so much that broadens our understandings of the doctrines of salvation. Without it, much of what is taught in other scriptures would not be nearly so plain and precious" (Ezra Taft Benson, "The Keystone of Our Religion," *Ensign*, January 1992, 5).

"The scriptures are rich in references to the Second Coming, an event eagerly awaited by the righteous and dreaded or denied by the wicked. The faithful of all ages have pondered the sequence and meaning of the many events prophesied to precede and follow this hinge point of history" (Dallin H. Oaks, "Preparation for the Second Coming," *Ensign*, May 2004, 7).

NOTES:

Time for scripture study requires a schedule that will be honored. Otherwise, blessings that matter most will be at the mercy of things that matter least.

—Russell M. Nelson, "Living by Scriptural Guidance," Ensign, November 2000.

LESSON THIRTEEN

JOURNALS: "OF FAR MORE WORTH THAN GOLD"

Hymns

No. 303, "Keep the Commandments"
No. 99, "Nearer, Dear Savior, to Thee"
No. 279, "Thy Holy Word"

SUMMARY:

1. Keeping a journal benefits ourselves, our posterity, and the Church. The record of this dispensation will be wanted in a future day. The Lord has taught that we need to keep true and faithful records. Although some feel journal keeping is a nuisance, we should remember that nothing is a nuisance when it is dictated by the Lord and when it brings forth good.

2. We should record in a journal God's blessings to us as well as our acts in the Church. Every woman should keep a brief history of her life and her dealings with God and with the Church. This should include recording blessings we have been given and our daily dealings with the Lord; this shows respect for God. Often, we do not realize the importance of events in our lives until later. When we record them in our journals, we can learn from them.

3. Children should learn to keep a journal early in life. Recording what takes place with them and around them will be a great blessing to

them and to their own future children. It is a great pleasure for children to reread their journals and be reminded of the good times they have had and how the Lord has blessed them.

QUOTES:

"I feel better about myself when I write in my journal. It makes me think of what I have done each day and plan for the future. When I write down a 'things to do' list in my journal, I seem to get more done. It is also sobering to realize that if I am going to leave my journal for my children and their children, then I had better live a life that is worthy to be remembered" (Roy B. Bennion, "Genealogy—Love That Transcends Time," *Ensign*, August 1987, 14).

"Writing in a journal is the best way to keep our personal history current. But a journal can best play its important role in our lives if we use it consistently. We might consider our journal as a map of our past, present, and future. We can look back to see where we have been, and then, with greater understanding and perspective, go forward, strengthened by our own experiences. In order for this to occur, we must record more than just our daily comings and goings—although a record of these experiences becomes a storehouse of cherished memories. We must express our feelings about the situations we experience—not just the events themselves" (Gawain and Gayle J. Wells, "Hidden Benefits of Keeping a History," *Ensign*, July 1986, 50).

"Accordingly, we urge our young people to begin today to write and keep records of all the important things in their own lives and also the lives of their antecedents in the event that their parents should fail to record all the important incidents in their own lives. Your own private journal should record the way you face up to challenges that beset you. Do not suppose life changes so much that your experiences will not be interesting to your posterity" (Spencer W. Kimball, "The Angels May

Quote from It," *New Era*, October 1975, 4–5).

HANDOUT:

Take five or ten minutes at the end of the lesson and have your sisters write a journal entry.

NOTES:

DATE:

LESSON FOURTEEN

REMEMBERING OUR SPIRITUAL HERITAGE

No. 30, "Come, Come, Ye Saints"
No. 35, "For the Strength of the Hills"
No. 36, "They, the Builders of the Nation"

SUMMARY:

From Zion's Camp to the trek to the Salt Lake Valley, the Saints endured many persecutions and trials but remained firm in the faith.

Zion's Camp:

Zion's Camp consisted of around two hundred men who gathered in Kirtland in 1834 to help redeem and rescue the Saints in Missouri. Due to their disobedience of the Prophet's counsel, they endured many hardships on their way to Missouri. When they arrived, a mob came from Jackson County and attempted to cross the Fishing River and destroy the men of Zion's Camp. However, just as the mob was about to advance on the camp, it was hindered by a great storm.

Far West, Missouri:

Saints who had been living in Jackson County were driven out of Missouri and into Illinois by Governor Boggs and his extermination order. The Lord, however, had commanded the Saints to lay the cornerstone of the temple in Far West. Despite the risk, members of the Quorum of the Twelve met in 1839 to dedicate the site according to the Lord's command. They were protected because they obeyed.

Commerce, Illinois:

Commerce became a refugee camp for the Saints fleeing from Missouri. As more and more gathered, there was less and less room for the Saints to settle. Many lived in their wagons or in tents and slept on the ground. This was a time of great illness, and because of the poor living conditions of the Saints in Commerce, many fell ill. One of the responsibilities of the Prophet was to look after the Saints. Although it was at great risk to his own health, the Joseph Smith went from small camp to small camp, healing by the power of the priesthood.

Arrival in the Salt Lake Valley:

Even though the Saints arriving in the Salt Lake Valley were tired and broken, they knew that they were to help fulfill the prophecy that the valley would become a great place where the Saints would build temples. Because of this knowledge, the Saints in the valley immediately began planting crops and building shelters. Because of their faithfulness, their labors were blessed. They knew nothing about the valley or the country that surrounded it, and they did not know the great loss and hardships the journey to the valley would bring them, but they knew that the Lord had revealed to His prophet the future of the Church and of the valley, and they followed the prophet diligently as they worked to establish the Church in the United States.

THE READY RESOURCE FOR RELIEF SOCIETY

QUOTES:

"We must be sure that the legacy of faith received from the pioneers who came before us is never lost. Let their heroic lives touch our hearts, and especially the hearts of our youth, so the fire of true testimony and unwavering love for the Lord and His Church will blaze brightly within each one of us as it did in our faithful pioneers. Their accomplishments were possible because they knew, as I know, that our Heavenly Father and His Beloved Son, Jesus Christ, restored the gospel of Jesus Christ through the Prophet Joseph Smith and that this Church will continue to roll forth until it fills the whole earth" (M. Russell Ballard, "Faith in Every Footstep," *Ensign*, November 1996, 25).

"Pioneers are still needed. A pioneer is described as one who goes before, preparing the way for others. He is a leader, first in his field in discovery and invention. He will be followed by settlers and developers who expand and exploit his discoveries. Anyone seeking to become a pioneer will take care to fill his mind with what is known about the route he plans to take. Some of the qualities needed in pioneering are interest, intelligence, imagination, and determination. A pioneer must investigate, plan, experiment, and work" (N. Eldon Tanner, "Pioneers Are Still Needed," *Ensign*, July 1976, 4).

HANDOUT:

Encourage your sisters to take a few moments when they get home from church to reflect on their heritage and fill out this family tree.

LESSON FOURTEEN

NOTES:

FAMILY TREE

ME

MY FATHER   MY MOTHER

GRANDFATHER   GRANDMOTHER   GRANDFATHER   GRANDMOTHER

GREAT-GRANDPARENTS

LESSON FIFTEEN

LIVING BY FAITH

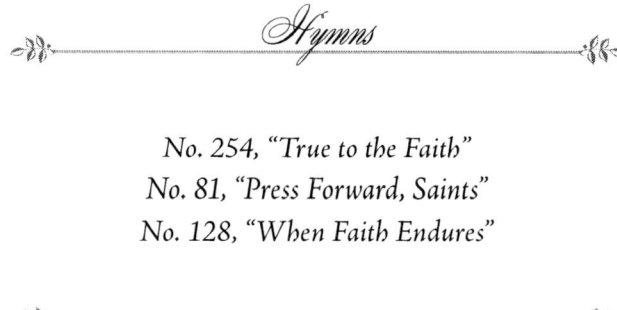

No. 254, "True to the Faith"
No. 81, "Press Forward, Saints"
No. 128, "When Faith Endures"

SUMMARY:

1. While in mortality we need to walk by faith; this is the first principle of the gospel. If we understood what the Lord has in store for us, we would be able to live by faith alone. All power is with God, and it is though Him that we are blessed. We must have faith that He guides and directs our lives.

2. We exercise our faith through our works and through the building of the kingdom of God. Faith is required of us to live our religion. In addition, we are required to do good works that correspond with our faith. When we have faith in God, we are more able to help Him build the kingdom with our works.

3. As we remain true to our covenants and to the Lord's commandments, God increases our capacity to have and to walk in faith. We need to live our religion truthfully and follow its principles. When we do this, we are more able to bring forth works of righteousness. When we are governed by the Spirit, our minds

are strengthened and our faith is increased. The Lord blesses those who show faith in Him and His guidance.

QUOTES:

"Great buildings were never constructed on uncertain foundations. Great causes were never brought to success by vacillating leaders. The gospel was never expounded to the convincing of others without certainty. Faith, which is of the very essence of personal conviction, has always been, and always must be, at the root of religious practice and endeavor" (Gordon B. Hinckley, "Faith: The Essence of True Religion," *Ensign*, October 1995, 2).

"Yes, this work requires sacrifice, it requires effort, it requires courage to speak out and faith to try. This cause does not need critics; it does not need doubters. It needs men and women of solemn purpose" (Gordon B. Hinckley, "'Be Not Afraid, Only Believe,'" *Ensign*, February 1996, 6).

"All the strength and force of man comes from his faith in things unseen. He who believes is strong. He who doubts is weak. Strong convictions precede great actions. Clear, deep, living convictions rule the world" (Robert L. Simpson, quoting James Freeman Clark, *Organizing for Eternity*, Brigham Young University Speeches of the Year, 20 April 1965).

NOTES:

> Peace, peace be unto you, because of your faith in my Well Beloved, who was from the foundation of the world.
>
> —Helaman 5:47

LESSON SIXTEEN

MARRIAGE AND PRIESTHOOD: PREPARING OUR FAMILIES FOR ETERNAL LIFE

Hymns

No. 300, "Families Can Be Together Forever"
No. 298, "Home Can Be a Heaven on Earth"
No. 294, "Love at Home"

SUMMARY:

1. The blessings of marriage and parenthood are far greater than worldly wealth. Marriage is ordained of God; unfortunately, the institution of marriage is failing in modern society. When choosing a spouse, we need to be more concerned with their standing with the Lord than with their standing with the world. Rather than follow the trends of society, we should realize that children are the choicest of blessings. Our families are eternal, and we must remember that they are a gift from God.

2. Children can learn to remain faithful in the Church through their parents' teachings. One of our duties upon this earth is to properly raise our children in the knowledge of the gospel. We should teach them Christlike ways through our example. Children are greatly blessed when they have parents to pray with them and to teach them to righteously live the gospel. If we teach them to pray, to honor God, and to walk uprightly, the Spirit will be with them,

LESSON SIXTEEN

and they will receive guidance and protection.

3. Parents should make their families their first priority. Fathers should preside in kindness and righteousness, and mother should teach and lead by example. Kindness, gentleness, and love are some of the best teaching tools. Fathers should utilize these principles as they stand at the head of their families. Mothers should understand that they give shape and character to their children. Children will learn from their mothers' examples. Mothers should teach their children to pray and to follow their examples.

QUOTES:

"Thank God for the joys of family life. I have often said there can be no genuine happiness separate and apart from a good home. The sweetest influences and associations of life are there" (Ezra Taft Benson, "Salvation—A Family Affair," *Ensign,* July 1992, 6).

"While few human challenges are greater than that of being good parents, few opportunities offer greater potential for joy. Surely no more important work is to be done in this world than preparing our children to be God-fearing, happy, honorable, and productive. Parents will find no more fulfilling happiness than to have their children honor them and their teachings. It is the glory of parenthood. John testified, 'I have no greater joy than to hear that my children walk in truth'" (James E. Faust, "A Thousand Threads of Love," *Ensign,* October 2005, 3).

"I simply reviewed my long-established priorities and said, 'I cannot seek the kingdom of God without loving and honoring *first* that family he has given to me. I cannot honor that family without loving and caring *first* for my wife!' I love her. She is my highest priority, and our eternal marriage in the temple is our highest commitment" (Neal A. Maxwell, "Peace and Love," *Ensign,* March 1979, 65).

HANDOUT:

Make a list on the chalkboard of ways to make a marriage more celestial. Have your sisters copy the list on this handout.

NOTES:

HOW CAN I MAKE MY MARRIAGE MORE CELESTIAL?

LESSON SEVENTEEN

TEMPLE WORK: TURNING OUR HEARTS TO OUR FAMILIES AND TO THE LORD

Hymns

No. 247, "We Love Thy House, O God"
No. 287, "Rise, Ye Saints, and Temples Enter"
No. 288, "How Beautiful Thy Temples, Lord"

SUMMARY:

1. Temple work prepares us, our ancestors, and our posterity to dwell with God. Temple work is a great blessing that allows us to prepare ourselves as well as others for eternal life. How ungrateful and unworthy we would be if we knew the blessings temples bring to us and we did not take advantage of them.

2. Family history and temple work seals us to our eternal families. The principles of the gospel are lasting after death, and they will bring our families together in the world to come. Because of the great principles of the gospel, we will be reunited with our families all the way back to Adam. We need to use our time on earth to trace our family histories as far as we can and seal our families together.

3. We need to spiritually prepare to complete temple work and receive the blessings of the temple. Before we go to the temple, we should go to the Lord and ask for the Spirit to prepare us to go to

LESSON SEVENTEEN

the temple and to learn. In addition, we need to go to the temple with pure hearts and minds. We should rid ourselves of unkind thoughts, confess our sins to the Lord and repent, and humble ourselves. When we are prepared to enter the temple to receive the wonderful blessings within, we will not be disappointed. The Spirit will teach us while we are there, and we will be better able to remain true when we leave the temple.

QUOTES:

"Let us truly be a temple-attending and a temple-loving people. We should hasten to the temple as frequently, yet prudently, as our personal circumstances allow. We should go not only for our kindred dead but also for the personal blessing of temple worship, for the sanctity and safety that is within those hallowed and consecrated walls. As we attend the temple, we learn more richly and deeply the purpose of life and the significance of the atoning sacrifice of the Lord Jesus Christ. Let us make the temple, with temple worship and temple covenants and temple marriage, our ultimate earthly goal and the supreme mortal experience" (Howard W. Hunter, "A Temple-Motivated People," *Ensign*, February 1995, 5).

"The Prophet Joseph taught that you and I are to become saviors on Mount Zion. We are to gather, build temples, seek after our dead, and perform all the vital ordinances. This work welds eternal links that bind us to each other and to our fathers. We are exalted as family units" (A. Theodore Tuttle, "Eternal Links that Bind," *Ensign*, May 1980, 40).

"In addition to physical preparation, we need to be prepared mentally and spiritually. Because the ordinances and covenants of the temple are sacred, we are under absolute obligation not to discuss outside the temple that which occurs in the temple. Sacred matters deserve sacred consideration" (Russell M. Nelson, "Prepare for Blessings of the Temple," *Ensign*, March 2002, 20).

HANDOUT:

Encourage your sisters to take this handout home and use it during family night to research an ancestor.

NOTES:

As a family, we can prepare the names of our ancestors for temple ordinances

Name: _____

Born: _____

Birthplace: _____

Married: _____ in _____

Died: _____ in _____

Baptized: _____

Endowed: _____

Sealed to spouse: _____

Sealed to parents: _____

LESSON EIGHTEEN

TEMPLE WORK: BECOMING SAVIORS ON MOUNT ZION

Hymns

No. 236, "Lord, Accept into Thy Kingdom"
No. 290, "Rejoice, Ye Saints of Latter Days"
No. 291, "Turn Your Hearts"

SUMMARY:

1. Heavenly Father is merciful and does not punish those who have not had the chance to receive the gospel on earth. The Lord is no respecter of persons, and He will not punish those who never had the chance to receive the gospel in this life. He has provided a way for them to receive the gospel through our temple work. They are taught in the spirit world, and we perform their sacred ordinances in their behalf. Then they are free to accept the gospel or reject it.

2. By building temples and doing temple work, we become saviors on Mount Zion. Those who have passed away cannot perform the ordinances of the gospel in the flesh, so we must become their proxies and perform the ordinances for them in the temple. Only in the temple are we able to complete this work. Vicarious work is what Christ did for us when He died for us. He laid down His life for our redemption because we could not do it ourselves. When we work in the temple, we become instruments in the hands of the Lord.

LESSON EIGHTEEN

3. The dead are eager for us to engage in temple work, and when we meet them in the spirit world, it will either be a day of joy or a day of sorrow and regret. Temple work is being watched with interest and great anxiety. We need to do the temple work so those in the spirit world can enjoy the same blessings we do. We should not stop working in the temple as long as we have the capability to do so. If we do not do temple work, which is required of us, we are under condemnation. When we pass away, we will sorrowfully meet others we could have helped redeem.

QUOTES:

"The Latter-day Saint view of the spirit world reveals that there is work being performed there. The most magnificent and extensive missionary program the mind can contemplate is centered in the spirit world. President Brigham Young declared: 'Compare those inhabitants on the earth who have heard the Gospel in our day, with the millions who have never heard it, or had the keys of salvation presented to them, and you will conclude at once as I do, that there is an almighty work to perform in the spirit world'" (Dale C. Mouritsen, "The Spirit World, Our Next Home," *Ensign*, January 1977, 51).

"Vicarious temple work for the dead more nearly approaches the vicarious sacrifice of the Savior Himself than any other work of which I know. No one comes with any expectation of thanks for the work which he or she does. It is given with love, without hope of compensation, or repayment. What a glorious principle!" (Gordon B. Hinckley, *Stand a Little Taller* [Salt Lake City: Eagle Gate, 2001], 25).

"I testify that much peace and joy can come into your life when you watch your children and grandchildren being baptized and then sealed to their families on behalf of your ancestors. I can only imagine the joy you will experience when you are greeted by your loved ones on the other side of the veil" (Mary Ellen Smoot, "Family History: A Work of Love," *Ensign*, March 1999, 18).

NOTES:

It is my prayer that we might understand our role in this great work and remain worthy to enter His holy temples. I know that if we will do this, the joyful day will come when we shall meet our ancestors once again and be able to say to them, "We did this for you."

—Elaine S. Dalton, "We Did This for You," *Ensign*, November 2004.

LESSON NINETEEN

FOLLOWING THE LIVING PROPHET

Hymns

No. 21, "Come, Listen to a Prophet's Voice"
No. 23, "We Ever Pray for Thee"
No. 25, "Now We'll Sing with One Accord"

SUMMARY:

1. From the beginning of the earth, God has sent prophets to reveal His will and to prepare and warn the inhabitants of the earth. God has never had a Church on this earth without a living oracle to receive revelation. Furthermore, the Lord would not have a man stand at the head of His Church unless that man were governed by revelation. If we pursue the counsels of the prophet, we will be on the straight and narrow path.

2. We sustain the living prophet by praying for him and by following his counsel. The prophet has an immense responsibility not only to the Church but also to the earth. His load is great. We can sustain the presidency of the Church with our faith, works, and prayers. We each need to bear our share of our own sins and failings; we each need to set our houses in order, do what is right, and lift others. By living righteously, we can strengthen and support the prophet.

3. We should not treat the counsel of the prophet lightly. We have the Holy Ghost to bear record of the truth of the prophet's words, and we know that the Lord governs the prophet's counsel. If we choose to live counter to the guidance of the Lord's mouthpiece, we will not prosper spiritually. We should also abandon all principles, theories, and practices contrary to prophetic counsel.

QUOTES:

"Among the members of the Church have been the living oracles of God, who have held the keys to direct this holy work. Without prophets, seers, and revelators, the Church and the kingdom of God cannot grow and prosper" (James E. Faust, "The Keys That Never Rust," *Ensign*, November 1994, 73).

"I do not believe members of this Church can be in full harmony with the Savior without sustaining His living prophet on the earth, the President of the Church. If we do not sustain the living prophet, whoever he may be, we die spiritually. Ironically, some have died spiritually by exclusively following prophets who have long been dead. Others equivocate in their support of living prophets, trying to lift themselves up by putting down the living prophets, however subtly" (James E. Faust, "Continuing Revelation," *Ensign*, August 1996, 5).

"Latter-day Saints should be able to accept the words of the prophets without having to wait for science to prove the validity of their words. We are most fortunate to have a living prophet at the head of the Church to guide us, and all who heed his counsel will be partakers of the promised blessings which will not be enjoyed by those who fail to accept his messages" (N. Eldon Tanner, "The Debate Is Over," *Ensign*, August 1979, 2).

NOTES:

And the arm of the Lord shall be revealed; and the day cometh that they who will not hear the voice of the Lord, neither the voice of his servants, neither give heed to the words of the prophets and apostles, shall be cut off from among the people.

—D&C 1:14

LESSON TWENTY

AGENCY: CHOOSING LIFE OR DEATH

Hymns

No. 239, "Choose the Right"
No. 260, "Who's on the Lord's Side?"
No. 237, "Do What Is Right"

SUMMARY:

1. God has given us agency, and we are responsible for our decisions to choose good or evil. God's plan for us allows us to choose right from wrong and allows our mind to be free to act for itself. With that blessing, we become responsible to Him for our acts. When our acts draw us closer to God, we are blessed; when our acts take us from the presence of the Lord, we inherit sore afflictions sooner or later. We cannot obtain happiness by breaking God's commandments.

2. We will be rewarded according to the law we choose to live. When we understand that our eternal happiness depends on the time we spend on earth, we will understand that it is not to our advantage to spend our time doing wrong. We cannot receive celestial glory by living a telestial life. In order to gain exaltation, we must live the principles of the gospel with faithfulness and put aside all selfishness and false principles.

LESSON TWENTY

3. Salvation is attainable if we follow the principles of conduct God has given us. There is only one way to God, and the rules and principles that govern that path are simple. Although this way may seem tough, the Lord does not require anything of us that we cannot perform without His help. If we pursue this course, we will be satisfied in this life and in the life to come. The more we adhere to the Lord's way and His gospel, the more He will sustain us in the journey.

QUOTES:

"The gift of agency is a crucial and fundamental element of our Father's great plan of happiness. Because we can exercise our agency only when alternate choices are possible, this plan involves considerable risks—the ability to make mistakes, to transgress divine laws, to disobey, to sin, and to rebel" (Spencer J. Condie, "Agency: The Gift of Choices," *Ensign*, September 1995, 16).

"If you want to reach your potential in the future, if you want to become the person the Lord wants you to be, you had better work on it today, because it is a true principle that we become what we do. If we want to be a successful university student, we had better be successful in high school. If we want to live a celestial life in the hereafter, we had better live a celestial life here on earth. Our futures are truly connected to our past" (Richard J. Maynes, "A Celestial Connection to Your Teenage Years," *Ensign*, November 1997, 30).

"Our Heavenly Father did not launch us on our eternal journey without providing the means whereby we could receive from Him God-given guidance to ensure our safe return at the end of life's great race. Yes, I speak of prayer. I speak, too, of the whisperings from that still, small voice within each of us; and I do not overlook the holy scriptures, written by mariners who successfully sailed the seas we too must cross"

(Thomas S. Monson, "Which Road Will You Travel?" *Ensign*, March 1991, 2–3).

HANDOUT:

At the end of the lesson, have your sisters fill out this chart. Have them make a list of their daily schedules and how they can use their agency to make choices that will bring them closer to their Savior.

NOTES:

My Daily Schedule

How I Can Improve My Daily Choices

LESSON TWENTY-ONE

FAITHFULLY ENDURING TRIALS AND OPPOSITION

No. 124, *"Be Still, My Soul"*
No. 129, *"Where Can I Turn for Peace?"*
No. 108, *"The Lord Is My Shepard"*

SUMMARY:

1. Trials and opposition provide experience and help us prepare for eternal life. We experience trials so we can be tried and tested to prove our integrity, our character, and our faith. While we may feel that our situations are unfair and that we are being overtested, the purpose of our trials will be revealed to us in the spirit world. The promise of eternal life can help us get through opposition.

2. In the great battle between darkness and light, God and His people will be victorious. The war that started in heaven continues on earth, and Satan is trying harder than ever to pull us to his side. He knows that he will not triumph in the end, so he tries to tempt us to leave God's presence. The Lord and His faithful people will triumph in the end, and we can use that knowledge to help us remain true.

3. The Lord watches over our lives if we are faithful, obedient, and humble. Jesus Christ died to redeem all people, and He watches

over us and is constantly helping us reach salvation. We cannot, however, enjoy His companionship and support if we are not keeping the commandments of God. The Lord is merciful unto us and will continue to guide and shape our lives so long as we come to Him for help and support. We must repent and humble ourselves so we can receive the Spirit in our lives and prepare to meet God.

QUOTES:

"Let us not presume that because the way is at times difficult and challenging, our Heavenly Father is not mindful of us. He is rubbing off our rough edges and sensitizing us for our great responsibilities ahead" (James E. Faust, "The Blessings of Adversity," *Ensign*, February 1998, 7).

"I am not prepared to say who will be on his [Satan's] side or how many he will have, but I am as sure as I live, by the inspiration of the Almighty, that the end of the conflict is as certain as the result at the beginning. That he fell in the beginning and was routed from heaven is a fact, and it also is a truth that no matter how many he shall gather on his side nor how bitter the conflict, he shall be defeated and banished from the earth and cast out of his own place. Christ will come to claim his own, to rule and reign" (Melvin J. Ballard, "Struggle for the Soul," *New Era*, March 1984, 35).

"Thus the promise is that in times of sorrow and affliction, if we endure and remain faithful and put our trust in him and are courageous, the Lord will visit us in our afflictions, strengthen us to carry our burdens and support us in our trials. He'll be with us to the end of our days, lift us at the last day to greater opportunities for service, and exalt us at last with him and reunited loved ones, and he will consecrate our afflictions to our gain" (Marion D. Hanks, "A Loving, Communicating God," *Ensign*, November 1992, 64).

NOTES:

TRIAL NUMBER FIVE

Carefully they laid
Out on the table
Trials one, two, three,
Four, five, and six.

"Choose one," they said.

"Oh, any," she cried, with a
　　horror
Born of the best of Halloweens,
"Any but number five.
It would kill me.
I promise you I would not
　　survive."

They thanked her graciously,
Escorted her out,
Then gift-wrapped, addressed,
And labeled "Special delivery"
Trial number five—

Sent with love from
Those whose assignment it is
To make sure you know
That you can go
Through trials one, two,
Three, four, ninety-nine,
Or five—
And, incredibly,
Come out alive.

—*Carol Lynn Pearson*, Beginnings and Beyond
(Springville, Utah: Cedar Fort, 2005), 176.

LESSON TWENTY-TWO

TEMPORAL AND SPIRITUAL LABOR, "HAND IN HAND TOGETHER"

No. 252, "Put Your Shoulder to the Wheel"
No. 243, "Let Us All Press On"
No. 223, "Have I Done Any Good?"

SUMMARY:

1. We have temporal duties to perform in the kingdom of God, and we should listen to the Lord's counsel regarding our temporal welfare. We cannot build up the kingdom of God by sitting in our homes. We need to build temples and churches, serve the children of the Lord, and take care of the needs of our families. If we could see the big picture, we would not be so concerned with wealth and material things. We need to humble ourselves and keep an eternal perspective so we can heed the prophet's counsel on temporal welfare.

2. Living the gospel includes our spiritual and temporal welfare, honest labor, paying an honest tithe, providing for our families, and staying out of debt. We should have a proper education, and we should see that our children receive a proper education as well because knowledge is all we can take with us into the spirit world. We need to honestly work and labor to provide for our families,

and we need to remember that the Lord is the one who truly provides for our families. We can respect the blessings He gives us by paying our tithes and offerings. In addition, we should avoid debt, which is a form of bondage.

3. Regardless of our wealth and material wants and needs, we must first pursue the kingdom of God. Many people would rather work and support themselves instead of supporting the Lord. All that we have and all that we will have comes directly from God. Nothing is wrong with riches so long as the seeker has first come unto God and sought His kingdom first. The wealth of this world will seem insignificant when we put the Lord first.

QUOTES:

"Next only to our devotion to God, the family comes first. Their temporal and spiritual well-being is of vital importance, and so there must be work to provide for it. This means hard work. Although there has to be a balance and time for the fun things, they cannot outweigh the need for a cooperative effort by all the members of the family to provide for their spiritual and temporal needs. To work is a commandment from God. It is the pattern for the happiness of individuals and the family and is the strength of both the Church and society" (William R. Bradford, "Unclutter Your Life," *Ensign*, May 1992, 28).

"Necessary debt should be incurred only after careful, thoughtful prayer and after obtaining the best possible advice. We need the discipline to stay well within our ability to pay. Wisely we have been counseled to avoid debt as we would avoid the plague" (L. Tom Perry, "'If Ye Are Prepared Ye Shall Not Fear,'" *Ensign*, November 1995, 36).

"So often it is the order of things that is fundamental in the Lord's instructions to us. The Lord is not telling us that we should not be prosperous. This would be inconsistent with the many records we have of Him blessing His people with prosperity. But He is telling us that we should seek prosperity only after we have sought and found Him. Then, because our hearts are right, because we love Him first and foremost, we will choose to invest the riches we obtain in building His kingdom" (L. Tom Perry, "United in Building the Kingdom of God," *Ensign*, May 1987, 34).

NOTES:

Work is honorable. It is good therapy for most problems. It is the antidote for worry. It is the equalizer for deficiency of native endowment. Work makes it possible for the average to approach genius. What we make lack in aptitude, we can make up in performance.

—J. Richard Clarke, "The Value of Work," *Ensign*, May 1982.

LESSON TWENTY-THREE

"OF ONE HEART AND ONE MIND"

No. 251, *"Behold! A Royal Army"*
No. 308, *"Love One Another"*
No. 246, *"Onward, Christian Soldiers"*

SUMMARY:

1. Unity prevails among the Godhead, and we as members of the Church need to seek that same unity. There has never been a division among Heavenly Father, Jesus Christ, or the Holy Ghost. They are one, always have been one, and always will be one; their objective and goal is also always the same. The presidency of the Church stands at the head. It is the link between God and His people. Unless we are unified, instruction from God, although passed from Him to His mouthpiece, will not reach His people.

2. Unity brings strength. Power comes in numbers, and a people united have a power that those who are divided cannot possess. With the Church growing rapidly, the need for unity among the leadership and the people of the Church is essential.

3. We need to unite in our doctrine, our labors in the kingdom, and our love for one another. The leadership of the Church, the missionaries, and the members all need to teach the same

doctrine. The fact that the doctrine comes from God and is given to one chosen leader to distribute among His people is one of the most beautiful parts of the gospel. If we do not labor as one in the kingdom, we will be scattered and lose the blessings of God. Furthermore, we must be of one heart and one mind and not allow anything to come between us and our love of God and His children.

QUOTES:

"It is the first principle of revealed religion to know the nature and kind of being that God is. As for us, 'we know [and testify] that there is a God in heaven, who is infinite and eternal, from everlasting to everlasting the same unchangeable God, the framer of heaven and earth, and all things which are in them' (D&C 20:17)" (Bruce R. McConkie, "The Lord God of the Restoration," *Ensign*, November 1980, 51).

"We of this Church can come to a unity and a oneness which will give us strength beyond anything we have yet enjoyed if we will obtain a sounder understanding of the principles of the gospel and come to a unity in our interpretations of present world conditions and trends. This we can do by prayerful study of the Lord's word, including that given to us through the living prophet" (Marion G. Romney, "Unity," *Ensign*, May 1983, 18).

"If we are to build Zion of which the prophets have spoken and of which the Lord has given mighty promise, we must set aside our consuming selfishness. We must rise about our love for comfort and ease, and in the very process of effort and struggle, even in our extremity, we shall become better acquainted with our God" (Gordon B. Hinckley, *Stand a Little Taller* [Salt Lake City: Eagle Gate, 2001], 187).

NOTES:

The leaders of Relief Society, Young Women, and Primary are all members of the ward and stake councils, and they have a unity which comes from their membership in Relief Society. To the degree that leaders ignore the contribution and influence of these sisters, in councils and in the home, the work of the priesthood itself is limited and weakened.

—Boyd K. Packer, "The Relief Society," Ensign, May 1998.

LESSON TWENTY-FOUR

PREPARING FOR THE SECOND COMING OF JESUS CHRIST

THE READY RESOURCE FOR RELIEF SOCIETY

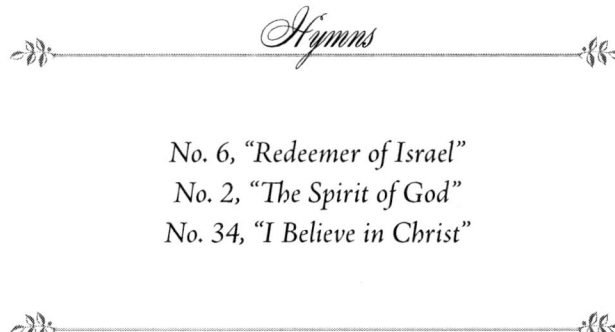

Hymns

No. 6, "Redeemer of Israel"
No. 2, "The Spirit of God"
No. 34, "I Believe in Christ"

SUMMARY:

1. In the last days, we must learn of the signs of the Lord's coming and watch for them. This is the last dispensation of this earth. If we want to know what is going to come to pass, we can read the prophecies in the scriptures. None of these prophecies will go unfulfilled. Because we do not know the hour of the Savior's return, we must study these signs prayerfully, and then we must watch for them faithfully so we can prepare for His coming.

2. We, as members of the Church, are responsible for preparing the way for Christ's return. The Lord has a great work ahead of us, and He is relying on us to shoulder that responsibility and complete that work. Temples need to be built, the gospel needs to be taught across the world, and members of the Church need to prepare themselves spiritually and temporally. The organization and membership of the Church will help members prepare for His coming.

LESSON TWENTY-FOUR

3. Not only must we prepare the way for Christ, but we must also prepare ourselves individually for His coming. Like the parable of the ten virgins, we need to be prepared to meet Christ. He will come in this dispensation. Nothing will stop the plans of God, so we need to make sure that as individuals we are ready to receive Him. We can prepare by keeping the commandments, praying, and building up God's kingdom on earth.

QUOTES:

"We believe that these severe, natural calamities are visited upon men by the Lord for the good of his children, to quicken their devotion to others, and to bring out their better natures, that they may love and serve him. We believe, further, that they are the heralds and tokens of his final judgment, and the schoolmasters to teach the people to prepare themselves by righteous living for the coming of the Savior to reign upon the earth, when every knee shall bow and every tongue confess that Jesus is the Christ" (*Teachings of Presidents of the Church: Joseph F. Smith* [Salt Lake City: The Church of Jesus Christ of Latter-day Saints, 1998], 44).

"But in the meantime, and as of now, the Lord has laid upon us the responsibility to lay the foundation for that which is to be. We have been commissioned to prepare a people for the second coming of the Son of Man. We have been called to preach the gospel to every nation and kindred and tongue and people. We have been commanded to lay the foundations of Zion and to get all things ready for the return of Him who shall again crown the Holy City with his presence and glory" (Bruce R. McConkie, "Come: Let Israel Build Zion," *Ensign*, May 1977, 116).

"What if the day of His coming were tomorrow? If we knew that we would meet the Lord tomorrow—through our premature death or through His unexpected coming—what would we do today? What confessions would we make? What practices would we discontinue?

What accounts would we settle? What forgiveness would we extend? What testimonies would we bear?

"If we would do those things then, why not now? Why not seek peace while peace can be obtained? If our lamps of preparation are drawn down, let us start immediately to replenish them.

"We need to make both temporal and spiritual preparation for the events prophesied at the time of the Second Coming. And the preparation most likely to be neglected is the one less visible and more difficult—the spiritual. A 72-hour kit of temporal supplies may prove valuable for earthly challenges, but, as the foolish virgins learned to their sorrow, a 24-hour kit of spiritual preparation is of greater and more enduring value" (Dallin H. Oaks, "Preparation for the Second Coming," *Ensign*, May 2004, 9).

HANDOUT:

Use this handout to make lists of ways to be spiritually prepared. Give your sisters suggestions such as: church attendance, personal prayers, family night, temple attendance, and so forth.

NOTES:

My Spiritual Preparedness Tool Kit

Church	Personal
Temple	Family

ABOUT THE AUTHOR

Kimberly Shaffer graduated from Brigham Young University with a bachelor's degree in marriage, family, and human development. She resides in Blue Springs, Missouri, and is pursuing a master's degree in ornamental horticulture. This is her first book.